The Book Bunch

Developing Book Clubs for Beginning Readers

Laura J. H. Smith

UpstartBooks

Fort Atkinson, Wisconsin

This work is dedicated to my literary past, present and future.

*To my parents, Dr. Sandra Wurth-Hough and the late
Dr. Lawrence Hough, who let me literally teethe on a book.*

＊

*To my husband, Dr. Paul Smith, who encouraged
and enabled me to write this work.*

＊

*To my daughters, Rebecca and Angela, who never cease
to remind me of the magic of the written word.*

Published by UpstartBooks
W5527 Highway 106
P.O. Box 800
Fort Atkinson, Wisconsin 53538-0800
1-800-448-4887

© Laura J. H. Smith, 2004
Cover design: Debra Neu Sletten

The paper used in this publication meets the minimum requirements of American
National Standard for Information Science — Permanence of Paper for Printed
Library Material. ANSI/NISO Z39.48-1992.

Table of Contents

Introduction

Groups have gathered to discuss the written word for as long as words have been printed on the page. People gather to delve into the characters created, explore settings developed by an author, uncover themes hidden among the words and obtain the opinions of others. This helps them increase their own personal knowledge and understanding of a piece of literature. However, this information quest is not confined to a certain age group. Even the earliest reader can benefit from gathering to share personal insights about a picture book. Some people might wonder why this is needed when the necessary skills are undeveloped and the attention span is too short to be beneficial; yet, by using the programs in this book you will discover that these arguments evaporate and a book club for first, second and third graders is truly a wondrous thing.

Book Club Goals

Teachers, librarians and parents realize that a love of reading and reading comprehension go hand in hand. A book club is an excellent means to introduce this link to first, second and third grade students. When children read a story they do more than look at the words on the page. They imagine the setting, visualize the characters, comprehend plot development and learn progression of events. If learning reading comprehension is fun, children will respond in a positive manner. Book clubs are an excellent way to make reading comprehension lively, exciting and fresh while accomplishing the following six goals.

Improve Reading Comprehension

Once children have determined that the squiggles on a page stand for letters and the letters for words, a child must learn what the words mean when they are put together. From this point, a child learns that the words form phrases that intertwine to provide information. The acquisition of these skills takes time and practice. Through group activity as well as individual thought, the themes, characters, plot and chronology of a story is reinforced time and time again and improves a child's understanding of a book.

Improve Vocabulary

If children only read at their present level, they will remain at that level. Only through stretching beyond this plateau and reaching higher, unexplored territory are new vocabulary words introduced. Additionally, learning what a word means by the context of the phrase teaches the ability to narrow down a meaning without having to constantly go to the dictionary or ask someone else. This empowers a child by instilling a sense of self-reliance. It can be attained through habitual introduction of new words and phrases.

Foster a Love of Reading

Reading is a difficult skill that not every child attains quickly and easily. The frustration behind learning to read can quickly turn into a "this isn't easy, I hate it" attitude. But the world tucked between a book's covers is well worth the reward. It is the responsibility of educators to coax children into the world of reading through the introduction of quality, fun and interesting pieces of literature.

Introduce Worlds Outside a Child's Comfort Zone

A child living in the Midwest has little idea what growing up in the urban Northeast is like. But through the world of books one can live someone else's life, if only for a moment. By introducing an unfamiliar setting to a child, you set the stage for discussing similarities and differences in a non-judgmental way, thereby decreasing the size of the world we live in.

Build Social Skills

Through working on craft projects and puzzles, a child learns how to share supplies and work together to solve a problem. Additionally, taking turns answering discussion questions and listening to what others have to say (as well as respecting what has been said) are all valuable lessons that a book club teaches.

Build Creativity

When children draw their favorite characters from a particular book, they must visualize what the character looks like and translate that image onto paper. Also, the process involved in selecting a favorite character builds decision-making skills. When the group shares what character they have selected, the verbalization of their decision requires a certain level of creativity. "I liked (name) because…" takes a large amount of thought, especially when there are several characters in a book.

Starting Your Book Club

When planning your book club, it is important to select proper titles. Any book can be talked about to some extent, but it is important to select books that are rich in plot, theme and characters in order to make the discussion lively and the process enjoyable for all. When selecting a book for discussion, you should consider:

- **Whether or not you enjoyed the book.** If you disliked the book, it will show, no matter how subtly, and influence the group's opinion. Children at this age have not developed the sense that it is acceptable for someone to dislike something that they enjoy. The conflicting emotions may undermine the lessons being taught.

- **Plot development and character portrayal.** Are the characters believable, real and interesting? Are negative stereotypes avoided? You might also look for a real-life lesson in the story and whether or not the story provides a window into a world outside the comfort zone of the reader.

- **The illustrations.** For younger readers, the pictures often tell as much if not more than the words written on the page. The expressions on a face or the color scheme used to create the setting often tell volumes more than the words. Therefore, it is vital when sharing a book with a child not to ignore the illustrations. "Read" the story by looking at only the illustrations. Do you know what is going on in the story? Could you "read" the story to a group using only the pictures? The bond between words and images is crucial in the success of a picture book for this age group.

When selecting a work for discussion, there are a few "should nots" that need to be addressed.

- **Do not select all books that have only a boy or only a girl as the main character.** It is part of the goal of a book club to introduce worlds outside the audience's realm of knowledge. But providing a few characters within the reader's comfort zone reinforces the validity of their own little piece of the world.

- **Do not select only books that are right at the child's reading level.** Provide a wide variety of levels. A book below the child's reading level may provide extra discussion as well as give the child a sense of pride in the fact that what was once difficult for him or her to understand is now "old hat." Likewise, a book above a child's reading level can stretch his or her abilities. If the story captures the child's interest, then the sense of achievement at being able to comprehend a book above his or her reading level will be priceless.

- **Not every work selected has to be of Caldecott or Newbery quality.** If there is a title that seems to be on the reading list of every child at school, it may be worth looking into and discussing.

How do you measure whether a person has increased their love of reading? That will require some additional observations. Does a child who started out saying very little all of a sudden provide insight in almost every discussion? Does that same child ask for other works by the author or on the same subject? Do you hear a child discuss a book outside of the discussion group? Have they recommended the book to someone else? These are all signs that a book was a success and that the love of reading is growing. As for reading comprehension, again, if a child increases his or her input during a book club and offers observations about the work, the skill is being built. Success can also be measured in repeat attendance when a book club is held outside of the classroom. If a child enjoys the program enough to return time and time again, regardless of his or her level of input, it is a good sign that he or she is learning something.

A Basic Book Club Program

A basic program consists of reading the story, doing an activity or craft to reinforce the story and discussing questions to provide a more in-depth study of the story. Feel free to personalize the following ideas to best fit your audience and flexibility.

Before Sharing the Book

- If time and resources allow, provide as many copies of each title as possible and distribute them among the students. Whether you provide copies for the students to read in advance of the meeting or if they simply refer back to the pages as the discussion occurs, having the pictures and words in front of them can jog an important observation as well as reinforce a key learning point.

- A student may come up with an observation not touched on by the discussion questions. Take this observation seriously and delve deeper into the idea if it is within the ground rules of the discussion group. Some students are linear thinkers and prefer to go step by step through an event while others are chaotic thinkers and opt for taking events out of order. Recognize these differences but maintain a linear approach as much as possible.

- The attention span of first, second and third graders is not lengthy. Keep the program moving! Start with introductions, ground rules and ice breakers. If the group does not know each other, provide name tags. Set ground rules at the very beginning but keep them positive. Ground rules might include: raise your hand, wait to be called upon and value the opinions of everyone. Be sure to keep the ground rules positive and go over them at every meeting. An ice breaker such as going around the room and saying your name and favorite book provides an introduction, as well as lets you learn a little more about your audience. Make sure you participate, too.

Share the Story

Read the story together and share the illustrations. Try to keep interruptions to a minimum by pointing out that the discussion will happen after the text has been read. This will allow those who have not had the opportunity to read the book a chance to fully synthesize the story.

Craft or Activity

The purpose of the craft or activity is to provide a fun, creative way to reinforce the theme of the story as well as give the children time to gather their thoughts and opinions of the story. Encourage discussion during this time. Sometimes, the children provide insights when they talk among themselves that would never come out when talking with an adult. Jot down any observations that might add to later discussion. If appropriate, allow time to share the projects. Not only will most children have a sense of pride in their creative efforts, but asking why they drew a particular character or pattern will encourage them to organize their thoughts and see a reason to an action.

Discuss the Story

Go through the book, page by page, with a discussion of what is going on. A linear discussion will prevent you from leaving out any points you wish to make about the text as well as teach cause and effect. Should anyone wish to skip ahead, praise the observation and ask the child to remember that point when the entire group reaches that event in the story. The main role of a book club leader is to guide the discussion by asking the questions, listen intently to the discussion and ensure that everyone is allowed to participate in the discussion. Once you have worked through the entire story, wrap up with any additional thoughts that have emerged. Now is a great time to ask who enjoyed the story and who did not. By leaving this question to the very end, children will not be influenced by the opinions of the others.

Snack Time

Finish up with a snack time. Snacks do not have to be anything elaborate—pretzels and juice are more than enough. In a public library setting this allows a break from the official discussion of the book and lets parents and guardians join in.

You will be surprised at how fast the time goes!

How to Use This Book

Now you are ready to start your book club! The following 27 programs include 26 titles and one summary program that can be used at the end of a programming season or school year. A wide selection of subjects, reading levels and book lengths are provided in order to keep students interested as well as to fit into the variety of programming timeslots an educator or librarian might have.

Amelia and Eleanor Go for a Ride

Pam Muñoz Ryan
Illustrated by Brian Selznick • Scholastic, 1999

A fictionalized account of a night when Amelia Earhart went to the White House to have dinner with Eleanor Roosevelt.

Story Evaluation

The story and puzzle are appropriate for any age group.

Storytime

Read the story with the group. If you flip past the recipe for Eleanor Roosevelt's pink clouds on angel food cake, you will see a real photograph from the trip discussed in this book. Point out that while we don't know every word that was said, the outline of the story is known. Also, don't forget to read the Author's Note before discussing the book with the class.

Group Activity

Amelia and Eleanor crossword puzzle. Have the children do the puzzle on page 13 independently, in pairs or as a group. If you choose to do the puzzle as a group, enlarge the blocks onto a piece of poster board.

Questions for Discussion

1. Why do you think Amelia and Eleanor were such good friends? What kinds of things did they have in common?

2. What was Amelia Earhart's claim to fame? How did this make her special?

3. Why did Amelia love to fly? How did it make her feel? Remember, this is a time when women weren't supposed to do things that men did.

4. What did Eleanor do that women, especially the first lady, were not supposed to do? How did driving make her feel? Was this the same feeling Amelia got when she flew an airplane?

5. Why didn't the secret service want Eleanor to go for a plane ride? Was it dangerous? Scary? Exciting?

6. What did Amelia and Eleanor do even before dessert was served? What was the trip like? Who was waiting for them when they returned?

7. Afterward, Amelia and Eleanor went back to the White House and had dessert, right? What did they do? Who drove the car?

8. What sorts of things can women do now that they were not supposed to do back when Eleanor drove and Amelia flew? Are there still adventures to be had?

9. Why do you think the illustrations look the way they do? Are they supposed to look like photographs?

Additional Activity

Instead of making the recipe at the end of the book, purchase pre-made angel food cake, whipped topping and strawberries with sugar. Enjoy this yummy dessert as a snack. Do remember to check with parents for allergies beforehand.

Amelia and Eleanor Go for a Ride
Crossword Puzzle

Across

2. Eleanor's husband was the _____ of the United States. *(senator, president, governor)*

4. What did Amelia and Eleanor go for a ride in? *(airplane, space shuttle, bicycle)*

7. Amelia and her husband were invited to dinner at the _____ House. *(Purple, Gray, White)*

Down

1. After returning from their flight, Amelia and Eleanor snuck away to _____ Eleanor's new car. *(drive, walk, skip)*

3. What was the present Amelia brought for Eleanor? *(teddy bear, card, scarf)*

5. The dessert served at the White House was _____ clouds on angel food cake. *(pink, blue, orange)*

6. Amelia Earhart was the first female pilot to fly solo across the _____ Ocean. *(Pacific, Indian, Atlantic)*

And the Dish Ran Away with the Spoon

Janet Stevens and Susan Stevens Crummel
Illustrated by Janet Stevens • Harcourt, 2001

One night, Dish and Spoon don't return after a reading of the famous nursery rhyme. Cow, Cat and Dog go on an adventure to bring Dish and Spoon back.

Story Evaluation

Third graders can read this story independently, second graders will need some assistance and first graders will need a lot of assistance. All ages will enjoy listening to the story and doing the activity.

Storytime

Read the story with the group.

Group Activity

Draw your favorite character. Supply paper plates, crayons and markers. Have each child draw his or her favorite character from the story on a plate. Go around the room and have the children share which character they drew and why.

Questions for Discussion

1. Who discovers that Dish and Spoon do not come back after the reading of the nursery rhyme? What does Cat do about it? What does Dog want to do?

2. Why is it important to get Dish and Spoon back? What do Cat, Cow and Dog do?

3. Who do Cat, Cow and Dog meet in the road? Who does Fork in the Road say he just saw wandering by? What does Fork in the Road do to help?

4. How many nursery rhymes and fairy tales are on Fork in the Road's map? What are they?

5. Where does Cow want to go first? Why does Fork in the Road say they shouldn't go see the Three Bears? Where does the group decide to go? What direction was it?

6. Who do Cat, Dog and Cow find at the haystack? What is Little Boy Blue doing? What does Dog do? Why does Dog sneeze?

7. What does Dog's sneeze do? Can Little Boy Blue help Dog, Cat and Cow find Dish and Spoon? Where do they go next?

8. Who helps Dog, Cat and Cow find Miss Muffet's house? Where does Spider tell them to look? What did Spider mean when he said that Wolf was very kind to strangers and that he was having some for lunch right now?

9. Where does the Big Bad Wolf live? Do Cow, Cat and Dog like going into the forest? How do they feel?

10. What does Wolf offer to do for Cat, Dog and Cow? Are they interested in a bath right then?

11. What does Dog find on the floor of Wolf's house?

12. What does Wolf try to do to Dog? Why does Dog say Wolf wouldn't want to eat her?

13. How does Cat save Dog? What happens to Wolf when Cat plays his fiddle?

14. Who do Cat, Dog and Cow hear once they escape from the Big Bad Wolf? Where do they think Dish and Spoon are now? Is it near or far? How do they get to such a far away place?

15. What happens to Dish and Spoon just as Cow, Cat and Dog arrive at the beanstalk?

16. Why does Spoon say they ran away? What does Dish say she wanted to do?

17. Why does Dog think Jack could put Dish back together again? Who had Jack already put back together?

18. What is Jack fixing when Dog, Cat, Cow, Spoon and Dish arrive? Why does the Blind Mouse have its tail cut off? Does Jack succeed in fixing Dish?

19. What happens after Dish is put back together? Does the rhyme stay the same? How does it change?

Brothers of the Knight

Debbie Allen • Illustrated by Kadir Nelson
Puffin, 2001

A modern retelling of the Twelve Dancing Princesses where the twelve sons of
Reverend Knight wear out their sneakers every single night.

Story Evaluation

First and second graders may need some assistance reading this story independently.
Third graders will not need any assistance. The craft will be enjoyed by all ages.

Storytime

Read the story with the group.

Group Activity

Make your own sneakers. Hand out photo-
copies of the sneaker worksheet on page 18
and crayons. Have the children decorate their
own pair of dancing shoes. After they finish
drawing, go around the room and have the
children share their artwork.

Questions for Discussion

1. Who is telling the story? Who is Happy? Are you surprised that a dog is telling the
   story? What does Happy have to say about that?

2. Who is your favorite brother? Is there a reason he is your favorite?

3. When you read the brothers' names, they have a rhythm (Brooke, Bobby, Joe,
   Snacky; Gerald and Jackie, Teeny Tiny Tappin' Theo; Lazy Leo—Big Fat Raoul likes
   to act a fool; Billie and Willie; Michael head of the clan, a ladies' man). Since this
   book is about dancing, be sure to point out the rhythm of the text. The words seem
   to dance off the page in places.

4. Why can't the Reverend keep a housekeeper?

5. Who is blamed for the brothers' shoes being "worn to threads, messed up, torn up,
   stinky, dirty, tacky, jacked up"? Did Happy do it?

6. What does the Reverend do about his sons' shoes?

7. Who comes to help the Reverend? What is Sunday like? Does she seem like someone you would want to be around? Why or why not?

8. What does Sunday make the boys do? Are they happy about it? What are they going to do to her?

9. Where do the boys go every night and what are they doing there? How does Reverend Knight feel about shoutin' and dancin'? Do you think the brothers are going to tell the Reverend where they were and why their shoes are "worn to threads, messed up, torn up, stinky, dirty, tacky, jacked up"?

10. How does Sunday follow the boys without them seeing her? How do the boys know she followed them?

11. Why do the boys not trust grown-ups? What is their reason? How does Sunday prove them wrong?

12. How does the Reverend find out about the closet of worn-out shoes? Who does he blame? What happens to Sunday?

13. What makes the brothers want to reveal what has been happening to their shoes?

14. What is the secret the Reverend has been keeping? How do the brothers discover that the Reverend knows how to dance?

15. What do the Reverend and the brothers do after they discover how much they all like dancing? Who do they have to go find?

16. Who is the only person unhappy about the wedding? Why?

Additional Idea

If you have access to the music for some of the dances mentioned, play it while the children are designing their dancing shoes. If you are feeling really adventurous, do a few of the dance steps while the music plays!

Brothers of the Knight
Design Your Own Sneakers

Use the crayons to decorate your own dancing shoes.

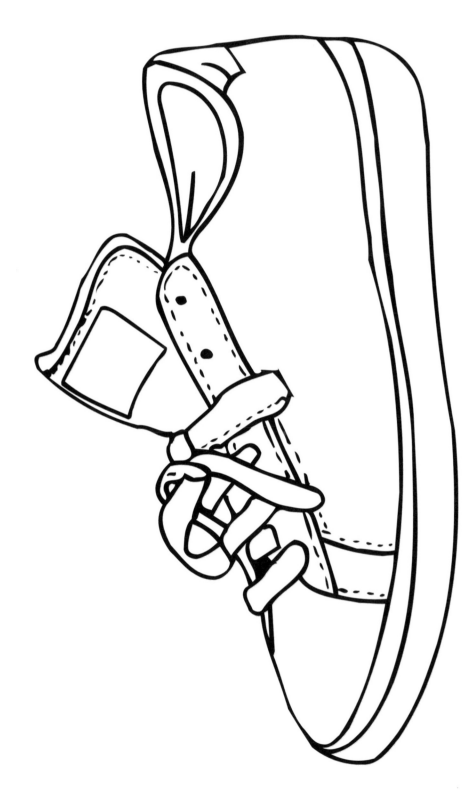

Casey at the Bat
A Ballad of the Republic Sung in the Year 1888
Ernest Lawrence Thayer • Illustrated by Christopher Bing • Handprint Books, 2000

The Caldecott Honor edition of the classic poem where Casey comes to bat in an effort to win the game for the Mudville Nine.

Story Evaluation

All ages will be able to read this story with minimal assistance and enjoy listening to it read aloud. The craft is appropriate for all ages.

Storytime

Before the children arrive, have two sets of index cards made, numbered one through the number of children in the club. Place the first set of cards in the chairs or in front of where the children will sit. Hand the second set to the children as they arrive. Have the children find their matching number. This helps them relate to using their ticket to find their seat at a real baseball game.

Read the story with the group. *Casey at the Bat* is intended to be read aloud. Even if the children read it before the discussion, be sure to read at least the corresponding quatrain as you move through the discussion questions.

Group Activity

Design your own baseball jersey. Photocopy the baseball jersey coloring sheet on page 21 for each child. Supply crayons and markers. Have the children design their own baseball jersey. What would they have on it if it were their own personal team? After they finish, go around the room and share what is on each jersey and why.

Questions for Discussion

1. "Casey at the Bat" is a ballad. What do you think a ballad is? Is it a poem? Is it a song? Is it a story and song together?

2. If the title did not include the date 1888, would you think this story took place today or long, long ago? What makes you think that? Look at the illustrations throughout the book.

3. In your own words, what happens in the first four lines of the story? What does the line "Cooney died at first, and Barrows did the same" mean? Who is winning the game?

4. If the crowd wants Casey to come to bat, why can't he? What is stopping him?

5. What does it mean that Flynn was a lulu and Jimmy Blake was a cake?

6. Is the crowd happy that there are two batters before Casey in the lineup? How unhappy are they?

7. Did Blake really tear the cover off the ball? What did he do? Is this an exaggeration? Do you ever use exaggeration to make a point? How?

8. Now that Blake and Flynn are on base, what does Casey have to do? What is the crowd's reaction?

9. What kind of player is Casey? Does he get nervous or scared when it's up to him to win? Who do you think is today's equivalent to Casey? This person doesn't have to be a baseball player, just someone expected to win the game when the team is behind.

10. What is the "leather-covered sphere"? How was it pitched? A slow ball? A curve? A fast ball? What makes you think so?

11. Does the crowd agree with the umpire's call on the first pitch? What does Casey do about it? What about the second pitch?

12. Up until the third pitch, there are four lines of poetry on every two pages. All of a sudden, there are only two lines for every two pages. Why do you think this is? Does it slow down the pace of the story and build the excitement?

13. What is it like in Mudville now? Why?

Casey at the Bat
Baseball Jersey

Design a baseball jersey for your own personal team.

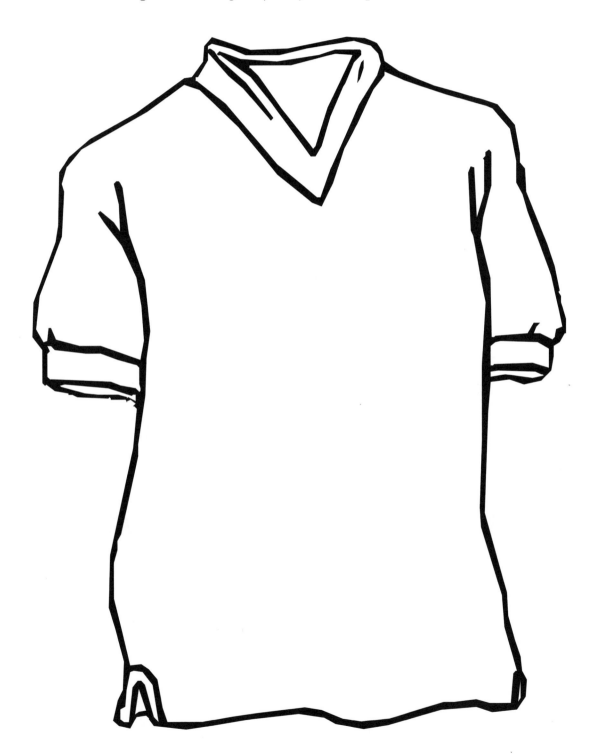

Click, Clack, Moo
Cows That Type
Doreen Cronin • Illustrated by Betsy Lewin
Simon & Schuster, 2000

Cows find an old typewriter and start making demands of Farmer Brown (including wanting electric blankets) or else they will produce no milk.

Story Evaluation

All ages can enjoy reading this story with minimal assistance. All ages will also be able to complete either of the group activities.

Storytime

Read the story with the group.

Group Activities

Make butter. Supply a mason jar with a lid and whipping cream. Place a small amount of whipping cream in the mason jar and seal tightly. Have the children shake the jar until small lumps form. These lumps are butter.

- Variation: Have two groups make butter. One group should shake the jar and the other group should roll the jar back and forth on the floor. Time how long it takes each group to turn the cream to butter. Please be sure to check for dairy allergies before introducing milk into the room.

Word Search. Have children do the Click, Clack, Moo Word Search on page 24.

Questions for Discussion

1. What is Farmer Brown's problem? What does he hear all day? How does this make him feel?

2. Does Farmer Brown think it is the cows typing at first?

3. What do the cows want? Why do they want electric blankets?

4. What does Farmer Brown say about the cows wanting electric blankets? Does he give them any?

5. What do the cows do when Farmer Brown refuses to give them electric blankets?

6. Who also wants electric blankets? What do the chickens do?

7. How does Farmer Brown feel about the chickens and cows going on strike? What does it mean to go on strike?

8. What does Farmer Brown do when the cows and chickens go on strike?

9. Who is a neutral party? What does he do? How does Duck help the cows and chickens?

10. What do the cows do about the ultimatum from Farmer Brown?

11. Who tries to eavesdrop while the cows are talking? Why can't they understand what the cows are saying?

12. What do the cows decide to do? What do they offer in exchange for the typewriter?

13. What does Farmer Brown decide to do?

14. Who is supposed to bring him the typewriter? What does Duck do with the type-writer? What do the ducks want? Do the ducks get what they want?

Click, Clack, Moo: Cows That Type
Word Search

Locate the words in the word bank. You will find the words up, down, across, diagonally or backwards.

```
C O W S R J X O H R C Z B L V
X A P E J L G W E G I D I I V
N A W M K R A T J N R U F Z J
M F V R E N I I K S T C S E D
K X P M S R A J I G C K N R W
C Y R O W X R L E G E H E G Y
S A O E M I L K B E L V K L H
F L P K C K O Q M M E W C E N
N Y T W R N J H U N S I I P K
T G K B M K N A G Y N Y H T S
Q N D L C W A L V G K G C X J
H R K I S G X D B C U Q A G Y
W G L G T B A R N P X Y C V R
J C U M G H H D K Q U A C K Z
V G B L A N K E T G K A X K G
```

Word Bank

BARN	CLICK	EGGS	MILK
BLANKET	COWS	ELECTRIC	QUACK
CHICKENS	DUCK	FARMER	TYPEWRITER

Cook-A-Doodle-Doo!

Janet Stevens and Susan Stevens Crummel
Illustrated by Janet Stevens • Harcourt, 1999

The Little Red Hen's great-grandson decides he is tired of chicken feed and follows in his famous relatives footsteps as he and his friends bake a strawberry shortcake.

Story Evaluation

This story can be read independently by third graders. Second graders may need some assistance and first graders will need significant help. All ages will enjoy hearing the story read aloud and can do both of the group activities.

Storytime

Read the story with the group.

Group Activities

Make strawberry shortcake. Supply pre-cooked shortcake rounds, frozen strawberries in syrup (thawed) and non-dairy whipped topping. *Note: strawberries are a high allergy food. Please check for any allergies before beginning this activity.* Discuss what order the shortcakes should be made and put them together at the same time. Talk about how they will taste just as good in any order, but the recipe in the book is cake, strawberries and cream.

Put events in order. Write key events from the story (such as Big Brown Rooster looking at a cookbook; Big Brown Rooster going to Dog, Cat and Goose for help; Pig burning his tongue trying to taste the hot cake) on index cards or pieces of paper. Scramble the events and have children put them back in order. You can put a small number on each piece just to remind yourself of what order they need to be in.

Questions for Discussion

1. Why does Big Brown Rooster decide to learn how to cook? What is he tired of eating? What makes him think he can become a great cook?

2. What does Big Brown Rooster decide to cook?

3. Who refuses to help Big Brown Rooster?

4. Who offers to help Big Brown Rooster? What can Turtle do? What can Iguana do? What can Potbellied Pig do?

5. Where does Big Brown Rooster put the apron? Is this where it goes? Do you think he knows anything about cooking? What about Iguana, Turtle and Potbellied Pig?

6. Does Iguana get the right kind of flour for the recipe? What do you call words that sound alike but are spelled differently and have different meanings?

7. Does Iguana sift the flour properly? What does he do wrong?

8. What does Pig want to do with the flour? Would it taste good by itself?

9. Where does Iguana look for the tablespoons? And the teaspoons? Is this the proper place?

10. Does Iguana get the right kind of stick? What does he get? What kind do they need?

11. How does Iguana want to cut the butter into the flour? Is this the right way? How should it be done?

12. How does Iguana want to beat the egg? What does he want to use? Is this the right way? How should it be done?

13. Once the cake is in the oven, what happens?

14. What happens to the cake once it is cooled and all done? Who drops it? Who eats it? How do the others feel about Pig eating all of their hard work? What do they suggest cooking next?

15. What do they finally decide to cook next? Will they mess up the kitchen this time? Why not?

16. What happens to the second shortcake? Who eats it all up?

Dumpling Soup

Jama Kim Rattigan • Illustrated by Lillian Hsu-Flanders • Little, Brown and Co., 1998

New Year's Day means dumplings to one Hawaiian girl. This year she gets to help for the very first time!

Story Evaluation

Third graders can read this story independently. Second graders may need some assistance and first graders may prefer to have the story read to them. All ages will enjoy the group activity.

Storytime

Read the story with the group.

Group Activity

Draw how your family celebrates New Year's Day.
Provide paper and crayons or markers. Have each child illustrate how he or she celebrates New Year's Day. After the children finish, go around the room and have them share their pictures.

We all get to wear new clothes.

Questions for Discussion

1. What does the narrator's family do every year on New Year's Eve? Who gets together? What do they do?

2. What does Grandma call the family? How does she feel about having such a diverse family? What does Grandma mean when she says "more spice"?

3. What goes into the dumpling mixture? Why is Grandma so particular about the recipe? What does she think the others need to do more of?

4. What will Marisa, the narrator, get to do to help?

5. What is mandoo?

6. How does Marisa feel about making the dumplings? What do her father and brother tell her to do?

7. What will brother Hiram do at Grandma's house?

8. Do all of Marisa's aunts make dumplings the same way? How are they made? Is one better than the other?

9. How do Marisa's dumplings turn out? How does she feel about them? What does Grandma tell her?

10. How do the other dumplings look? What happens to all of the dumplings?

11. Who does the official taste testing? How does Father react?

12. What happens when Marisa's dumplings are cooked? What does Grandma do with them? What does Marisa fear?

13. What does *Wahiawa* (WAH-hee-ah-wah) mean? What happens when the Yang family gets together?

14. What covers Grandma's steps? Why are lots of shoes on the porch? Where did the shoes come from? What do the children do with the shoes?

15. According to Grandma, what will happen if you fall asleep before midnight?

16. What is the favorite game among the grandchildren?

17. Why do they shoot off fireworks at midnight?

18. Why do they eat dumpling soup as the first meal of the New Year? What does Hiram say Marisa's dumplings look like? How does the family feel about the dumplings?

Gila Monsters Meet You at the Airport

Marjorie Weinman Sharmat • Illustrated by Byron Barton • Simon & Schuster, 1990

A boy from New York City moves west where he fears buffalo stampedes, killer cacti and gila monsters await.

Story Evaluation

Second and third graders can read this story independently. First graders may need assistance with a few words. All ages will enjoy the group activity, though the mess level may vary.

Storytime

Read the story with the group.

Group Activity

Sand painting. Supply colored sand, glue, water, paintbrushes, newspaper to cover tables, card stock or cardboard squares, bowls, plastic spoons and pencils. Place the colored sand in individual bowls and put a spoon in each bowl. Put the glue in bowls and thin it with a small amount of water. Have the children sketch a southwestern scene on a piece of card stock cardboard. The pictures do not have to be extremely detailed. Give them examples of mountains, horses, cacti, gila monsters, etc. Then have the children pick parts of their pictures to which they want to apply a certain color of sand. Have them paint glue on these parts and apply one color of sand with a spoon. Tap the extra sand back into bowl. Repeat until the scene is complete.

Questions for Discussion

1. What is the name of the boy who tells the story? Are we ever told his name? Is this important? Could he be any kid who doesn't want to move?

2. Where does the narrator live at the beginning of the story? Does he want to move? Why or why not?

3. What scares the narrator about moving out west? How does he think westerners talk? How do they dress? What do they eat? What will he miss eating?

4. What does the narrator think out west is like? Is it entirely a desert? What does a map of the area look like?

5. Who is Seymour? According to Seymour, who meets you at the airport? How does the narrator know this is a fact? Can you always believe what you read in a book?

6. Who does the narrator meet at the airport? What does he think the kid's name is? Why does he think the kid's name is Tex?

7. Where is Tex moving? How does Tex feel about it? What does Tex think he will find in the East? How is the weather back east?

8. How do people live in the East according to Tex?

9. Who or what lives in the sewers in the East? What happens to the alligators? What do they do?

10. Once the narrator gets into the taxi to go to his new home, what does he see? Does he see gila monsters? Does he find something familiar—like what he knew in New York City?

Goin' Someplace Special

Patricia C. McKissack • Illustrated by Jerry Pinkney • Simon & Schuster, 2001

Set in 1950s Nashville, 'Tricia Ann travels across town to find the one place that is completely integrated—the public library.

Story Evaluation

Third graders can read this story independently. Second graders will need some assistance. First graders will need significant assistance and would probably benefit from listening to the story read aloud first. All ages will enjoy hearing the story read aloud. The activities are appropriate for all ages, but first graders may need extra assistance.

Storytime

Read the story with the group.

Group Activities

Make a book. Supply cardboard, heavy gift wrap or brown paper, white paper, stapler, scissors, glue, crayons and markers. For each book, cut a piece of gift wrap or brown paper to 11 x 14 inches and cut two pieces of cardboard to 4½ x 6 inches each. Have the children lay their gift wrap or brown paper face down on the table. Cover the cardboard pieces with glue. Lay them centered and approximately ¾ inch apart on the paper. Fold over the edges of paper, glue them down. If the children would like, have them cover the inside of the cardboard with the same paper. Fold several sheets of white paper in half. Place the fold in the gap between the pieces of cardboard. Close the book and staple the edges. If the children used brown paper, have them illustrate the outside of their book.

Draw your someplace special. Supply paper, crayons and markers. Have the children think of someplace that is special for them—someplace that means a lot to them or a place that they always look forward to visiting. After the children have drawn this place, go around the room and have them share what they have drawn.

Questions for Discussion

1. What is 'Tricia Ann's "someplace special"? Why does she enjoy going there? How does she feel about it?

2. What is Mama Frances's concern about 'Tricia Ann going alone? How does she tell 'Tricia Ann to act?

3. What does Mama Frances mean when she tells 'Tricia Ann to "hold yo' head up and act like you b'long to somebody"?

4. What is the first stage of 'Tricia Ann's trip? Where does she have to sit on the bus? What is the Jim Crow sign? How does she feel about sitting in the back of the bus?

5. What has Mama Frances told 'Tricia Ann about the signs?

6. Who is Mrs. Grannell? Where does she sit? What does Mrs. Grannell tell 'Tricia Ann when she gets off the bus? What does she mean?

7. How does 'Tricia Ann feel about the Peace Fountain? What does she do there? Why does she get up from the bench when it was obvious that she was tired and needed a rest? How does she feel about the Whites Only sign?

8. Who does 'Tricia Ann meet next? What does Jimmy Lee give her? Why does she say she was so upset? Who in 'Tricia Ann's family worked on the Peace Fountain?

9. What does Jimmy Lee say about Monroe's Restaurant? Why doesn't he want to eat there anyway? What advice does Jimmy Lee give 'Tricia Ann?

10. Who is Mr. John Willis? What does the Southland Hotel's doorman tell her?

11. How does 'Tricia Ann get inside of the Southland Hotel's grand lobby? How does the manager make her feel? Does she want to go inside?

12. Where does 'Tricia Ann run? Does she feel like going "someplace special" is worth all the trouble?

13. Who does 'Tricia Ann meet at the Mission Church gardens? Who is Blooming Mary? What advice does she have?

14. What does 'Tricia Ann hear when she stops to listen? What had 'Tricia Ann's grandma taught her? Is she going to go back home or "someplace special"?

15. What happens in front of the Grand Music Palace? Where would 'Tricia Ann have to sit if she was going to a show there? What is the Buzzard's Roost? Is that someplace you'd want to sit? Where does Hickey want to go after 'Tricia Ann leaves?

16. Where is "someplace special"? What about it makes it so special to 'Tricia Ann? What had Mama Frances called it?

Gregory, the Terrible Eater

Mitchell Sharmat • Illustrated by Jose Aruego and Ariane Dewey • Scholastic, 1983

Gregory, a goat, prefers to eat people food (vegetables, fruits, etc.) instead of goat food (tin cans, wax paper, shoelaces).

Story Evaluation

All ages should be able to read this story independently and will enjoy listening to the story as it is read aloud. Both activities are appropriate for all age groups.

Storytime

Read the story with the group.

Group Activities

Recycle art. Supply large pieces of construction paper, magazines, food coupons and newspapers. Have the children glue pictures of food torn from magazines and coupons to a piece of construction paper. They will make a collage of their favorite foods. Have the children show and tell their meals. Discuss why certain choices were made. Did they pick their favorite foods? Why did they not pick certain things?

Food groups game. On poster board or a blackboard, write the four main food groups (Dairy, Grains, Meats and Proteins, Fruits and Vegetables). Briefly discuss what each group is. The object of the game is to place the food under the appropriate heading. On an index card, write the names of the foods listed on page 34 and others you may think of. Be sure to include some items (like pizza) that could go under more than one heading. If you have pictures of the foods, by all means use them! Deal the cards out to the children. Go around the room and have the children put their cards under the right heading. This is not about who gets the most right answers. Other children can help if someone gets stumped.

Possible choices:

cheese	pizza	yogurt
beans	spaghetti	pita bread
tomatoes	ice cream	cucumber
bread	apple	hamburger
glass of milk	grapes	fish

Questions for Discussion

1. Is Gregory an average goat? What makes him different?

2. Have your parents ever wanted you to eat something you didn't want to eat? Did you try it? Did you like it after you tried it?

3. What do Gregory's parents do about his eating problem? What does Dr. Ram recommend doing with such a picky eater? What sorts of meals were Gregory's parents supposed to serve?

4. How do Gregory's parents introduce goat food into Gregory's diet? Does spaghetti and a shoelace in tomato sauce with string beans and a rubber heel cut into small pieces sound like a good meal? What would you give Gregory to eat?

5. What happens after Gregory starts liking goat food? What does he start eating? Is this a good idea? Why? Why not?

6. What do Gregory's parents do to cure Gregory of eating everything in sight? Does it work? What happened?

7. What does Gregory learn about food? Have you ever eaten too much? How does it make you feel?

Journey to Freedom
A Story of the Underground Railroad
Courtni C. Wright • Illustrated by Gershom Griffith • Holiday House, 1998

Harriet Tubman leads a group of slaves from Kentucky to Canada and freedom.

Story Evaluation

Second and third graders should be able to read this story independently. First graders may find the story too long to read independently, but will enjoy hearing it read aloud. The group activity is appropriate for all age groups.

Storytime

Read the story with the group.

Group Activity

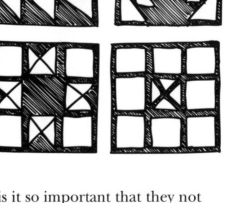

Make a freedom quilt. Supply solid pieces of black construction paper; triangles, squares and rectangles cut from brightly colored construction paper; and glue sticks. Have the children design their own freedom quilt using the black paper as a background and gluing the brightly colored triangles, squares and rectangles on it.

Questions for Discussion

1. Mama tells Joshua and Nathan to be quiet. Why is it so important that they not make a sound? What could happen if they are loud?

2. Who is leading Joshua's family to Canada? Who was Harriet Tubman?

3. Why does Harriet Tubman want the group to move quickly? What sort of danger are they in?

4. What will happen if the family is captured and returned to Master Grant?

5. What do Joshua and the others do when they hear barking dogs? What could the dogs mean?

6. Are the dogs part of a search party? What kind of dogs are these? What do Joshua's father and some of the other men do to get rid of the dogs?

7. Why do people call Harriet Tubman "Moses"?

8. What is the Underground Railroad?

9. What is so important about a quilt having the color black in it?

10. Why does Joshua's family want to go to Canada? What will they find there? What do they hope to find in Canada?

11. Has it been an easy trip for Joshua and his family? What has happened? Is it worth it to them to continue the trip?

12. Why doesn't Harriet want it to snow? What happens when it does snow?

13. Why does the group have to stay in the shelter instead of continuing on once the snow stops?

14. Once the group reaches the next station, Mr. Nelson tells them they will be in Ohio the next day. Why do they have to continue on to Canada instead of staying in Ohio? What does the Fugitive Slave Act say?

15. How does the group get from Ohio into Canada? Does Mama enjoy the boat ride across Lake Erie?

16. What happens once the group crosses Lake Erie? Do they like being free? What does it mean to them to be free?

Just the Two of Us

Will Smith • Illustrated by Kadir Nelson
Scholastic, 2000

A father's song of love to his son. ***Note:*** *This is Will Smith's homage to fathers who are there for their children. A father figure does not have to be biological. This work provides a strong, positive male image and role model.*

Story Evaluation

Second and third graders can read this story independently. First graders may need some assistance. All ages will enjoy hearing this story and doing the group activity.

Storytime

Read the story with the group.

Group Activity

I want to be an astronaut on the spaceshuttle.

What do you want to be? Have the children draw the answer to this question, "If you could be anything you wanted to be, what would it be?" Supply white paper, crayons and markers. After the children finish their illustrations, go around the room and have them share their drawings.

Questions for Discussion

1. How does the father feel as he is holding his newborn son? Is he happy? Worried? Scared? Is it possible to feel all of these emotions at one time?

2. Why does it take an hour for the father to get the car seat right on that first night?

3. What do you think the castles in the sky are? *(Yes, very esoteric, but the answers might surprise you.)*

4. Have the father's feelings changed when the little boy turns five years old?

5. Do you see any rhyming words on this page? (e.g., comedy/me, tall/all, be/MC, time/line, etc.)

6. What does the father mean when he says "I don't mind if you lose, as long as you came with it"?

7. Even though the father's marriage ends, does he still love his son? Why?

8. Do you think the dad really knows where the CD-ROM is supposed to go on his computer? What makes you think that?

9. Why is the boy mad at the other boy? (Look at the outstretched arms—he's holding the boy's hat.) Does the father want him to fight? How does the boy feel? What is the father's advice?

10. How does the father feel about his growing son? Is that love ever going to change?

Katie and the Sunflowers

James Mayhew • Scholastic, 2001

One rainy day, Katie and Grandma go to the museum. While there, five classic paintings come to life—with disastrous consequences.

Story Evaluation

Older readers will be able to enjoy this story independently, but everyone will enjoy the adventure. The craft is for all ages.

Storytime

Read the story with the group.

Group Activity

Make your own van Gogh *Sunflowers*. Supply sunflower seeds in the shell, yellow construction paper, construction paper for the background, crayons or markers and glue. Have the children use sunflower seeds for the center and pieces of yellow construction paper torn into pieces for petals. They can use crayons or markers to embellish their artwork if they desire.

Questions for Discussion

1. What is Katie's favorite painting? Why does she like van Gogh's *Sunflowers*?

2. What happens when Katie touches the painting?

3. Who laughs at Katie when the flowers fall out of the painting? What are the girls' names?

4. Why won't Masie and Musette help? Under what conditions does Mimi say she will help?

5. Who is Zazou? What does he do with the sunflowers Katie and Mimi gather?

6. Who does Zazou run into? What does the waiter do?

7. How do Mimi and Katie get away from the waiter? Do you remember the name of the painting they reached into? What happened to the tablecloth, apples and oranges in Cézanne's *Still Life with Apples and Oranges*? What happens to the waiter when he catches up to Mimi and Katie?

8. Where does Zazou go to get away from the waiter? Who does Zazou see in *Tahitian Pastorals* by Paul Gauguin? What does Zazou do about the dog in the painting?

9. What is it like on the island of Tahiti? Is it rainy like outside the museum? What does Katie want to do in the painting to cool off?

10. What does Zazou find on the beach? What are the Tahitian women going to do with the pirate treasure? What do they do with the gold?

11. How do Katie and Mimi find their way back to the painting *Sunflowers?* Who left the trail of sunflower seeds?

12. Do Katie and Mimi leave the museum paintings in a mess after their adventure? What did they do?

13. Who is waiting for them in front of *Café Terrace at Night?* What "present" does the waiter have for Katie and Mimi? What does Katie do about the bill? How does the waiter react?

14. What does Katie keep from one of the pictures? What do you think she is going to do with the sunflower seeds?

Library Lil

Suzanne Williams • Illustrated by Steven Kellogg • Puffin, 2001

This is a modern tall tale about a super librarian, Lil, and how she turns a town on to reading and confronts the biker bad boy, Bust-'em-up Bill.

Story Evaluation

Third graders can read this story independently. Second grade students may need assistance and first graders may find it a little long. All ages will enjoy hearing this story read aloud. The Word Search is appropriate for all age groups.

Storytime

Before reading the story, ask the group what they think a librarian is. What are they like? What do they do? What do they look like? (This introduces the concept of a stereotype.) Explain that (more than likely) a lot of what they have described is a stereotype.

Read the story with the group.

Group Activity

Word Search. The Word Search on page 43 uses key words from the story. It can be done independently or as a group. Go over the answers together.

Questions for Discussion

1. Introduce the concept of a tall tale. (Talk about what it is, the element of exaggerated truth, etc.) Give examples of Paul Bunyan, John Henry, Pecos Bill and others. How does Library Lil compare to these tall-tale characters?

2. What type of librarian is Lil? Does she act like other librarians? What would you expect if you were to meet her on the street?

3. How does Library Lil feel when no one comes to her storytelling festival? How do you know this? Is it in the text or the pictures?

4. What are the townspeople doing instead of coming to the library? What is Library Lil's opinion of what the townspeople were doing?

5. What stopped the townspeople from watching so much television?

6. What do the people do for the two weeks after the storm when the power is out? Once the power is restored, do they go back to watching television? What do they do?

7. What do you think happened to all of the televisions that were no longer being used?

8. Who is Bust-'em-up Bill? How do you think he got that name?

9. Is Bust-'em-up Bill happy that he can't watch his favorite program on television? What is his favorite program? What does Bust-'em-up Bill do when he can't watch his favorite program?

10. Do you think Bust-'em-up Bill and his gang know how strong Library Lil is when they park their motorcycles in the Bookmobile's parking space? What were they expecting?

11. Does Bust-'em-up Bill think he is going to have to read a book when he challenges Library Lil to move all their motorcycles? What does he make his gang do when Library Lil does move the motorcycles?

12. What book does the gang get into a fight over? Is *The Mouse and the Motorcycle* a real story or a made-up one? (This is a great opportunity to introduce a copy of *The Mouse and the Motorcycle*.)

13. What happens to Bust-'em-up Bill after he reads a book? Does he like reading? If so, how much?

14. What happens to Bust-'em-up Bill and Library Lil after the story ends? *(If you have a copy with a dust jacket, it shows Lil and Bill on top of a wedding cake.)*

Library Lil
Word Search

Locate the words in the word bank. You will find the words up, down, across, diagonally or backwards.

```
O  B  S  Y  B  L  F  D  D  L  M  I  J  E  N
X  Z  U  O  I  I  B  O  L  D  W  C  W  L  O
F  W  O  L  Z  S  V  I  H  N  B  L  B  C  I
R  K  O  G  R  X  B  W  K  I  Y  Z  C  Y  S
S  O  M  U  A  I  Z  B  W  Q  P  X  H  C  I
N  N  R  O  D  G  C  S  T  M  M  U  E  R  V
S  T  O  R  Y  T  E  L  L  I  N  G  S  O  E
M  L  D  T  P  L  I  B  R  A  R  Y  T  T  L
Q  F  I  Q  U  U  J  H  L  I  H  B  E  O  E
T  A  W  L  O  M  P  A  R  P  U  D  R  M  T
P  E  G  T  J  B  H  P  L  N  W  N  V  F  F
B  L  S  T  O  R  M  V  E  N  B  C  I  Q  Y
O  N  A  D  C  U  O  U  O  T  H  P  L  F  G
B  O  O  K  M  O  B  I  L  E  S  X  L  F  F
O  A  Q  S  Y  J  L  H  U  N  H  A  E  V  A
```

Word Bank

BILL	CHESTERVILLE	MOTORCYCLE	STORYTELLING
BOOKMOBILE	LIBRARY	PUPPETS	TELEVISION
BOOKS	LIL	STORM	

Mailing May

Michael O. Tunnell • Illustrated by Ted Rand
HarperCollins, 2000

There isn't enough money for a train ticket to Grandma Mary's, so five-year-old Charlotte May Perstorff, with the help of fifty-three cents worth of stamps, is mailed from Grangeville to Lewiston, Idaho.

Story Evaluation

Second and third graders should be able to read this story independently. First graders will need minimal assistance. All age groups will be able to enjoy the craft with assistance.

Storytime

Read the story with the group. Explain that this story is based on a real event. This is called historical fiction. Even though we do not know exactly what happened, we know bits and pieces.

Group Activity

Make a snow globe. For each child, supply a baby food jar (or other small clear glass jar with lid), plastic figurine and florist clay. Set out white glitter and cold water for the children to share. Have the children attach the figure to the lid of the jar with florist clay (be sure they use plenty so the figure doesn't come off after the jar is sealed). Fill the jar with water to within ½ inch of the top. Add 1 tablespoon of glitter. Place the lid tightly on the jar. Have an adult seal the jar with a hot glue gun or florist clay.

Questions for Discussion

1. Does Grandma Mary really live a million miles away? Why does May think it is that far away? Is this an exaggeration? Why does May exaggerate? Have you ever exaggerated about something you have wanted to do or see? When? Why?

2. Why can't May go visit her Grandma? How does this make her feel?

3. What does May do when she finds out there isn't enough money to send her to Grandma Mary's house?

4. Why can't May get a job at Alexander's Department Store? How does this make her feel? How do you know this without seeing a picture of May? What does it mean to "slog" your way home?

5. What is happening when Ma and Pa whisper back and forth? Is it a surprise? How does May feel when she is told to come along and ask no questions?

6. Where do Pa and May go? What is Pa's plan?

7. What does the postal code say about mailing girls? What is May classified as? How big of a baby chick is she?

8. What does May do while riding in the mail car? Is she alone? Who watches after her?

9. Is it an uneventful trip? What happens that makes May stop dead in her tracks?

10. How does Mr. Harry Morris react to the fact that May was a package, not a passenger?

11. What happens once May gets to the Lewiston railroad station?

Many Moons

James Thurber • Illustrated by Marc Simont
Harcourt, 1998

Princess Lenore wants the moon, and what a princess wants, a princess gets. The King consults his wise men on how to get the moon for the Princess, but it is only after the clever Jester hears the problem that a solution is devised.

Story Evaluation

Third graders can read the story independently, second graders will need minimal assistance and first graders will need significant assistance. All ages will enjoy listening to the story and doing the activity.

Storytime

Read the story with the group.

Group Activity

Moon pendant. Supply a 1–2" Styrofoam ball (one per person), glow in the dark paint, glitter or glitter pens, paper plates, paper clips (one per ball), lanyard or string and newspaper to cover the tables. Have the children push the paper clip into the Styrofoam so it forms a loop. Squirt a generous amount of glow in the dark paint onto a paper plate. Roll the ball in the paint until it is covered. Sprinkle the wet paint with glitter or let it dry and decorate with glitter pens. Thread lanyard or string through the loop.

Questions for Discussion

1. What do you think a surfeit of raspberry tarts is? How can you tell what a word means if you don't already know?

2. Do you think the Lord High Chamberlain is as wise as he looks? Why? How would you describe him?

3. According to the Lord High Chamberlain, how far away is the moon? How big is it? What is it made of?

4. Who comes after the Lord High Chamberlain?

5. What kind of magic has the Royal Wizard done for the King? Was it always successful?

6. According to the Royal Wizard, how far away is the moon? How big is it? What is it made of?

7. Who comes after the Royal Wizard?

8. Do you think the Royal Mathematician really figured out how far is Up? Or how long it takes to get away? Why do you think he says he has figured out such things? Does it make him look smarter?

9. According to the Royal Mathematician, how far away is the moon? What is it made of? How big is it?

10. Why does the King send for the Court Jester if the wisest men in the kingdom can't get the moon for Princess Lenore? What does the King want the Court Jester to do?

11. What does the Court Jester suggest be done about getting the moon for the Princess?

12. How big does Princess Lenore say the moon is? How far away is it? What is it made of?

13. What does the Court Jester do after he finds out all about the moon?

14. How does the Princess Lenore feel after receiving the moon on a chain?

15. What problem does the King foresee when night falls? Who does he want to solve the problem?

16. What does the Lord High Chamberlain suggest to do in order to prevent Princess Lenore from seeing the moon in the sky? What is wrong with this plan?

17. What does the Royal Wizard suggest doing? What is wrong with this plan?

18. What does the Royal Mathematician suggest doing? What is wrong with this plan?

19. What does the Court Jester do after the King tells him about the other plans?

20. What is Princess Lenore's answer to why the moon is in the sky?

21. Who is the wisest person in this story? Why?

Matzah Ball
A Passover Story
Mindy Avra Portnoy • Illustrated by Katherine Janus Kahn • Kar-Ben Publishing, 1995

Aaron cannot pass up the chance to go see his favorite baseball team, the Baltimore Orioles, play. But it's Passover and that means no popcorn, peanuts or cracker jacks, which significantly dampens the mood—until he meets someone who completely understands.

Story Evaluation

Third graders should be able to read this story independently. First and second graders will need some assistance. All ages will enjoy hearing the story read aloud and doing the activity.

Storytime

Read the story with the group.

Group Activity

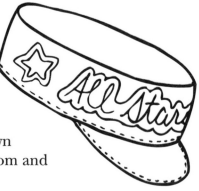

Design your own baseball cap. Supply painter's caps from a home improvement store, markers, glitter pens and fabric paint. Have the children design their own baseball cap. What would they have on it if it were their own personal team? After they have finished, go around the room and have them share what is on their cap and why.

Questions for Discussion

1. Who has tickets to the Orioles game? How does Aaron feel about going? Who puts a damper on his spirits? Why?

2. How does Aaron feel about not being able to eat pretzels, ice cream or Cracker Jacks? Is it easy for him to be Jewish? What does he want?

3. What does Aaron eat for lunch at the ballpark? Does Larry think it is bad to bring his own lunch? What does Larry want from Aaron?

4. What happens to Aaron's lunch at the ballpark? Who eats most of his dessert? Is he upset about this? Why or why not?

5. How was the game? Who liked matzah? What does Aaron do with it?

6. What does Aaron fantasize doing? Why?

7. How is Aaron feeling? Is he enjoying the game? Why or why not?

8. Who interrupts Aaron's self-pity party? What does the old man tell him?

9. Where does Aaron fantasize he is? Does that make him feel better?

10. Is Aaron able to focus on the game after talking with the old man? What happens to the home run ball? Where does the old man go?

11. How do Aaron's friends feel about him catching the ball? What do they tell him?

12. Who is the old man? How does he know Aaron's name? How can you explain what happened?

Mice and Beans

Pam Muñoz Ryan • Illustrated by Joe Cepeda
Scholastic, 2001

Grandmother Rosa María prepares her house for Catalina's birthday party complete with cake, decorations, piñata and, of course, rice and beans. Everything will be perfect as long as there are no mice around, or so Rosa María thinks.

Story Evaluation

Third graders can read this story independently, second graders will need minimal assistance and first graders will need average assistance. All ages will enjoy listening to this story aloud and doing the craft.

Storytime

Read the story with the group.

Group Activity

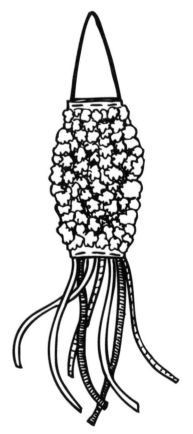

Mini-piñatas. Supply toilet paper or paper towel tubes (one for each child), stapler, tissue paper, glue, paintbrushes, water, small bowls, glitter pens or glitter glue *(optional)* and goodies to go inside piñata *(optional)*. Thin the glue with water in the small bowls. Have the children use a paintbrush to paint a thin layer of glue onto the paper roll. Then they can tear pieces of brightly colored tissue paper and apply them to the roll. The tissue paper can be applied flat or be bunched up to create texture. Streamers are also a nice touch. Cover the entire roll. Have the children use a glitter pen to write their name on the outside of their piñata. If you have them, place goodies inside the piñatas and staple each end shut.

Questions for Discussion

1. What is going to happen at Rosa María's house? Why isn't Rosa María worried about the size of her home?

2. What is wrong with having a mouse around?

3. What does Rosa María do on Sunday? What do you think happens to the mousetrap she put out the night before? What makes you think that?

4. On Monday, what happens to Rosa María's twenty-fourth napkin? Who took it? Was it the same thing that took her mousetrap?

5. What happens to the mousetrap on Tuesday? What does Rosa María think happened to the mousetrap?

6. What happens to the piñata's feathers? Why do you think the mice are taking things?

7. Where does Rosa María's *bolsa* go? What is a *bolsa*? Who took it? Why do the mice need a pocketbook?

8. Does Rosa María really forget everything that was missing? (The spoon, the bolsa, the mousetraps, the napkin, the candles?) What does she really forget?

9. Who makes sure the candy is put in the piñata? Why?

10. What is Little Catalina's present?

11. How does Rosa María discover the mice? How does she feel about finding them? What does she decide to do?

12. Why do the mice need all of the things they took? What do they do with them?

Moses Goes to a Concert

Isaac Millman • Farrar, Straus and Giroux, 2002

Moses, a deaf child, goes to a concert with his classmates and meets the percussionist in the orchestra who also happens to be deaf.

Story Evaluation

Second and third graders can read this story independently. First graders will need minimal assistance. All ages will enjoy listening to the story read aloud and doing the activity.

Storytime

Read the story with the group. If at all possible, have someone sign the entire story while it is read and teach the children some of the hand signs.

Group Activity

Make a drum or maracas. Supply an oatmeal box, coffee can, concentrated juice can (with lid) or chip can per person; construction paper; scissors; crayons or markers; dried beans; and scotch tape or glue. Have the children cut a piece of construction paper to fit around their box or can. Tape or glue the paper to the outside of the container. Use crayons or markers to decorate the outside of the container. If they are making maracas, they can add beans to the inside of the container and seal the lid. If they are making a drum, leave the beans out.

Questions for Discussion

1. How does Moses feel the vibrations when he plays the drum? How does removing his shoes help Moses feel the vibrations of the drum? Why does Moses want to feel the vibrations?

2. Where is Moses's class going on a field trip?

3. Who does Mr. Samuels know in the orchestra? What does this friend do?

4. Why do some of Moses's classmates wave instead of clap? (*To the hearing-impaired, waving is the same as clapping.*)

5. What shocks Moses when the percussionist comes out? Why isn't she wearing shoes?

6. How do Moses and his classmates "hear" the concert? What do the balloons do?

7. What is the surprise Mr. Samuels has for each student? What can they do with the balloons?

8. What does the percussionist tell them after the concert? Why did she want to become a percussionist even after becoming deaf?

9. What do the children do after meeting the percussionist? Do they enjoy playing on the instruments?

10. What does Moses want to be when he grows up? Does he think he will succeed? Why?

A New Barker in the House

Tomie dePaola • Putnam, 2002

Morgan and Moffie have a new brother, Marcos, and are anxious to take him to show-and-tell. But three-year-old Marcos only speaks Spanish and Morgan and Moffie only speak English.

Story Evaluation

All age groups will enjoy this story, but younger children may require some assistance with the Word Search.

Storytime

Read the story with the group.

Group Activity

Two-part puzzle. Have the children complete the Word Search on page 56, then match the English word to the Spanish equivalent on page 57. If your group is not familiar with word searches, have them work together in groups of two or three.

Questions for Discussion

1. What is the surprise Mama and Papa have for Moffie and Morgie? Are they happy about the new child? How old do they think the child will be? How old is Marcos?

2. Does Marcos speak English? What language does he speak? How do Moffie and Morgie feel about having to teach Marcos English?

3. What kind of questions do Moffie and Morgie have about Marcos? Do they know how tall he is or what he looks like?

4. What does Moffie want to do with her new brother?

5. What does Morgie want to do with his new brother?

6. What do both Morgie and Moffie want to do with Marcos?

7. What do Morgie and Moffie think of Marcos when he says *"Hola"*? What do they do when Papa reminds them that Marcos only speaks Spanish?

8. What does Moffie do with Marcos? How does Marcos react?

9. What does Morgie do with Marcos? How does Marcos react to the dinosaurs?

10. Why can't Marcos play ball? What does Marcos do?

11. Where does Moffie want Marcos to sleep? Where does Morgie want Marcos to sleep? What do Morgie and Moffie do when Marcos sleeps in his own room?

12. What does Marcos do once Morgie and Moffie leave the room? What stays in the bed with him?

13. The next morning, does Marcos like the Dino Pops and the Alphabet Bits? What does he do with the cereals? What does Mama do about Marcos not liking the cereals? Does Marcos like the toast with jelly, orange and glass of milk she serves?

14. How does Marcos react when the twins come home from school? Why does he not want to play with them? What does Marcos like to play with? What do Moffie, Morgie and Marcos play with together?

15. What does Marcos call himself at dinner that night? What does Markie call Moffie and Morgie? What are they all together?

A New Barker in the House
Word Search

Locate the words in the word bank. You may find the words across or up and down.

```
F  A  M  I  L  I  A  S  M  T  J  H  O  L  A
F  I  X  C  O  L  U  M  P  I  O  O  G  P  S
Y  V  L  B  A  L  L  I  J  P  F  G  Y  E  A
H  Y  B  H  O  U  C  H  K  A  K  I  F  L  I
E  T  R  A  M  N  O  F  A  M  I  L  Y  O  Z
R  B  O  X  V  A  N  S  E  E  S  A  W  T  S
M  E  T  Z  W  C  E  M  S  L  I  D  E  A  I
A  F  H  O  M  O  J  T  O  Q  L  Y  T  E  S
N  A  E  M  G  J  I  S  C  H  R  D  O  A  T
A  A  R  Z  K  J  T  I  A  E  D  X  B  S  E
B  U  N  N  Y  N  O  C  J  L  E  O  O  B  R
T  D  E  L  L  P  A  R  M  L  L  Q  G  C  E
S  U  B  I  B  A  J  A  E  O  N  J  A  M  O
S  W  I  N  G  W  L  I  E  G  H  O  N  S  Z
B  U  Q  F  L  O  V  H  E  R  M  A  N  O  W
```

Word Bank

BALL	FAMILIA	HOLA	SLIDE
BROTHER	FAMILY	PELOTA	SUBIBAJA
BUNNY	HELLO	SEESAW	SWING
COLUMPIO	HERMANA	SISTER	TOBOGAN
CONEJITO	HERMANO		

A New Barker in the House
Spanish to English Words

Match the Spanish word to the English word with the same meaning.

Spanish	English
Hola	Slide
Familia	Swing
Pelota	Brother
Conejito	Hello
Tobogan	Bunny
Columpio	Sister
Subibaja	Family
Hermana	Seesaw
Hermano	Ball

New Cat

Yangsook Choi • Farrar, Straus and Giroux, 1999

New Cat lives in a tofu factory in the Bronx where she is very happy—except when it comes to the little mouse in the production room (the one place New Cat isn't supposed to go). But one night, New Cat trusts her instincts instead of her training and saves the tofu factory from a mouse-induced fire.

Story Evaluation

All grades can read this story with minimal assistance.

Storytime

Read the story with the group.

Group Activity

Clay cats. Supply clay and Popsicle sticks. Give each child a lump of clay to form his or her own cat. Have them use the Popsicle sticks to create details (fur, faces, etc.) on the animals.

Questions for Discussion

1. Look at the first picture (where New Cat is sitting at the president's desk). From looking at this picture, who do you think is in charge of the factory? Does New Cat feel like she is in charge?

2. Who is Mr. Kim? How does he get along with New Cat?

3. How did Mr. Kim come to own New Cat? How did New Cat get her name?

4. What does Mr. Kim make at the factory? What are New Cat's jobs at the factory? What is the most important job?

5. What is the one thing New Cat doesn't like about her job? Why doesn't she like the little mouse? Where does the mouse live? Why does this bother New Cat?

6. When the mouse runs into the production room and New Cat finds that the door is not completely closed, what does she do? How does she feel about finding the door open?

7. What is the mouse doing in the production room? Is this dangerous? What does New Cat do?

8. What happens after the mouse chews through the electrical wires? What is the bright orange light? Does New Cat like the orange light? Why not? What does New Cat do to try to escape the orange light? What happens?

9. Why doesn't the entire factory burn to the ground? What stops the fire? How does the tofu spill? Why does Mr. Kim say that it makes sense that the fire was stopped by the tofu?

10. Where does Mr. Kim look for New Cat? Was she there? How does Mr. Kim feel when he can't find New Cat? How long have they been friends? Where does Mr. Kim find New Cat? Are Mr. Kim and New Cat happy to see each other?

11. What does Mr. Kim do to prevent mice in the production room? What does New Cat do after the big adventure? What does Mr. Kim do?

Owl Moon

Jane Yolen • Illustrated by John Schoenherr
Philomel, 1987

A young girl and her father go out one cold dark night and look for owls.

Story Evaluation

Second and third graders can read this story independently. First graders will need some assistance. The craft is appropriate for all ages.

Storytime

Read the story with the group.

Group Activity

Pinecone owl. Supply one pinecone per child, feathers, construction paper, glue and one small square of heavy cardboard per child. Before the children arrive, glue the flat end of the pinecone to the square of cardboard. Let dry. This will provide a sturdy base for the pinecone creations. Have the children use construction paper to create eyes, ears and a beak for their owl. The children can simply tear the paper instead of using scissors if desired. Have them glue feathers to their owls for decoration.

Questions for Discussion

1. What is owling? Why do the little girl and her father want to find owls?

2. What do the trees look like? The moon? What does the train whistle sound like? What kind of night is being described? Is it a hot summer? A cold winter? How do you know?

3. How do the dogs react to the train whistle? What do they do? How does the narrator feel when the train whistle and dogs fade away?

4. What kind of noise do their feet make? What are their shadows like?

5. Why does the little girl have to be quiet? How does she feel about finally being able to go owling?

6. How does Pa call the owls? What kind of owl does he sound like? Do they get a response? How does the little girl feel? Is she upset? Why or why not?

7. How does it feel to go owling? Is it toasty warm? Icy cold? What does it mean to be "cold and hot at the same time"? Does the little girl complain? Why or why not?

8. What kind of place is the woods? Is the little girl scared to be in the woods?

9. Do you remember how the clearing looked? Is it a busy place? A quiet, pristine place?

10. What happens the next time Pa calls out to the owls? What does Pa do?

11. What do they see then? What does the shadow do? What is the shadow? How long do they look at each other?

12. What does Pa say they ought to do once the owl flies away? Now that the little girl can talk, does she? What does she call herself?

13. What is the only thing you need to go owling? How does the little girl feel to have seen an owl?

Porkenstein

Kathryn Lasky • Illustrated by David Jarvis
Scholastic, 2002

Dr. Smart Pig doesn't want to go trick or treating alone and decides to create a new friend who is wolf-proof.

Story Evaluation

This story can be read with minimal assistance by all ages.

Storytime

Read the story with the group.

Group Activity

Make a Porkenstein mask. Supply a sheet of pink fun foam (one per mask), scissors, string, hole punch and glue. Cut a circle out of the foam, one for each child. Cut eye holes large enough to ensure the child can see properly. Have the children use scraps of fun foam to create the snout and ears. Glue the snout and ears onto the mask. Use markers to create a mouth, scars, warts, etc., on the mask. Punch holes on either side of the mask and thread string through holes. Tie the string to fit each child's head.

Questions for Discussion

1. Who is Dr. Smart Pig? Why doesn't he have any friends? What happened to his brothers?

2. What does Dr. Smart Pig decide to do about not having a friend? What qualities does he want to create in a friend? Why?

3. What does Dr. Pig create first? What is wrong with his creation? What does Dr. Pig do about it?

4. What is Dr. Pig's second creation? What is wrong with the pig bat? What does Dr. Pig do about it? What ingredient does he add to his concoction?

5. What is Dr. Pig's third creation? What does the giant pig say to Dr. Pig? What does the giant pig want? How does Dr. Pig feel about his creation eating so much? What does the pig end up eating? What does Dr. Pig name his creation?

6. Who is excited about the creation of a giant pig? What does the Big Bad Wolf want to do with Porkenstein?

7. Who does Dr. Pig think has shown up at his door just after sunset? How does he react when he sees who it really is? What does the wolf do when Porkenstein comes to the door?

8. What does Dr. Pig think happened when he hears a scuffle, a gulp and a rumbling belch? What really happened? How does Dr. Pig feel when he discovers Porkenstein ate the wolf?

9. Does Dr. Pig consider Porkenstein to be an invention? Was he happy to have a friend?

10. What does Porkenstein suggest they do? What does Porkenstein dress up as? What does Dr. Pig dress up as? Do they have a good time trick or treating? What makes you think so?

Sam and the Tigers
A New Telling of Little Black Sambo

Julius Lester • Illustrated by Jerry Pinkney
Puffin, 2000

Sam collects the finest clothes only to lose them piece by piece to hungry tigers who threaten to eat him. Using his wits, Sam not only prevents getting eaten, but also gets his fine threads back.

Story Evaluation

Third graders can read this story independently and second graders will need some assistance. First graders may need more time and aid in reading the story, but will enjoy listening to it read aloud. All ages will enjoy both activities.

Storytime

Read the story with the group.

Group Activities

Make butter. See page 22 for directions.

Tiger masks. Supply paper plates, crayons or markers, scissors, hole punches and string. Cut eyeholes in the paper plates. Make sure they are large enough for the child to see well. Have the children design tiger faces on their masks. Punch holes into each side of the mask. Tie a piece of string to each side of mask. Tie it off so it fits the child's head.

Questions for Discussion

1. What is so strange about people's names in Sam-sam-sa-mara? Would it be confusing for everyone to have the same name?

2. What is the relationship between people and animals in Sam-sam-sa-mara? Do they think it is strange to live and work together?

3. What do you think habiliments are? Why does Mr. Elephant pick such a big word to mean clothes?

4. What kind of clothes do Sam's mom and dad pick out at Mr. Elephant's Elegant Habiliments? How does Sam react to the brown jacket and white shirt?

5. What kind of coat does Sam pick out? Is it a dull red? A bright red? What kind of red? What tells you this?

6. What does Sam find at Monkey's Magnificent Attire? What shade of purple are the pants?

7. What kind of shirt does Sam find at The Feline's Finest Finery? What color is the shirt?

8. What kind of shoes does Sam pick out at Mr. Giraffe's Genuine Stupendous Footwear Emporium? What does it mean that they were silver, "shining like promises that are always kept"?

9. Is Sam finished shopping? What does he pick out next? What color would you call "green as a satisfied mind"?

10. What do you think Sam's parents thought of the clothes? What do they do to protect their eyes? Who do they say Sam will put out of business?

11. How does Sam feel about his new clothes? Is he pleased? Disappointed?

12. What happens to all of Sam's clothes on the way to school? How does each tiger react to getting a piece of clothing? Do they react the same way Sam did when they were first purchased?

13. What does Sam tell the tiger that took his shoes? Where should the tiger wear the shoes since he has four feet and only two shoes?

14. Once Sam loses all of his clothes, what does he do? What stops him from crying? What is he afraid will happen? Are the tigers going to come back and eat him? What are the tigers arguing about? What do the tigers do after they stop arguing?

15. Do the tigers hear Sam when he picks up his clothes? What are they doing? What happens to the tigers when they finally see Sam has his clothes back? Can they stop running in circles? What eventually happens to the tigers?

16. What does Sam do with the butter that the tigers turn into? Does Sam tell anyone where the butter came from?

17. Why does Sam eat 169 pancakes?

The True Story of the 3 Little Pigs

Jon Scieszka • Illustrated by Lane Smith
Puffin, 1996

The wolf tells his side of the story of the three little pigs in an effort to clear his name.

Story Evaluation

This story will be enjoyed by all ages but independent reading is best reserved for third graders. All ages will enjoy the activity.

Storytime

Read a traditional version of "The Three Little Pigs." Then read this story to the group. Ask the children to think about the differences and similarities between the two stories while they do the activity.

Group Activity

Wolf and Pig puppets. Supply brown paper bags, glue sticks or scotch tape, crayons or markers, brown construction paper (for wolf ears and tail), pink construction paper (for pig ears and nose), short pieces of pink yarn (one tail per pig) and large googly-eyes (two per puppet) *(optional)*. Have each child tear colored construction paper into ear, nose and tail shapes, depending upon which animal he or she is making. Have the children use a glue stick or scotch tape to attach the body parts. Attach googly-eyes to the puppets. The children can use the crayons or markers to create clothes for each animal.

Questions for Discussion

1. A narrator is a person who tells the story. Who is telling this story? Why does he want to tell the story?

2. What does the wolf say the real story of "The Three Little Pigs" is about?

3. Why is the wolf sneezing?

4. Why does the wolf need a cup of sugar?

5. What happens to the first little pig's straw house, according to the wolf?

6. What happens to the second little pig's house of sticks, according to the wolf?

7. What makes the wolf so mad at the third little pig's house? What does he do about it?

8. How does the wolf end up in jail?

9. Do you believe the wolf's side of the story or the traditional telling? Why? Why do you believe one telling rather than the other?

10. Does the wolf deserve to be in jail? Why or why not?

Young Cam Jansen and the Missing Cookie

David A. Adler • Illustrated by Susanna Natti
Puffin, 1998

Junior detective Cam Jansen must discover who took Jason's chocolate chip cookie.

Story Evaluation

Second and third graders can read this story independently. First graders will need some assistance. The Word Search is a simple introduction to such puzzles.

Storytime

Read the story with the group.

Group Activity

Word Search. Have the children complete the Word Search puzzle on page 69.

Questions for Discussion

1. Why does Cam close her eyes and say, "Click"?

2. How does Cam prove to Jason that she has memorized the homework problems without writing them down?

3. Does Jason believe that Cam has a photographic memory? What does he do to test her?

4. Why is her name Cam? What is it a nickname for? What is her real name?

5. What is missing from Jason's lunch box? What kind of cookie was it?

6. Who is the first suspect? Why is she a suspect? Why do they rule out Pam?

7. Who is the second suspect? Why is she a suspect? What kind of cookie was she eating?

8. What does Cam want to remember when she closes her eyes and says, "Click"?

9. Who is the third suspect?

10. Why does Cam stop Jason from accusing Annie? What does she see in Jason's lunch box that tells her Annie didn't steal his cookie?

11. Who ate the cookie? How do they know?

Young Cam Jansen and the Missing Cookie
Word Search

Locate the words in the word bank. You will find the words down, across or diagonally.

```
P  C  A  M  E  R  A  M  K  V  C  L  Z  T  W
X  H  D  P  G  Q  Y  I  L  S  C  G  B  X  W
I  D  O  M  Q  R  Y  S  B  K  N  Z  N  J  Y
J  J  U  T  R  R  I  S  M  S  M  T  E  O  C
K  F  D  C  O  R  C  I  B  D  W  I  Y  Y  I
C  X  K  N  D  G  J  N  D  T  K  N  E  K  Y
S  C  H  O  O  L  R  G  G  O  A  D  G  N  J
D  O  G  J  Y  Y  J  A  O  V  K  D  E  H  A
X  A  Y  E  M  F  S  C  P  W  S  W  U  F  S
E  Z  D  Y  W  P  R  A  I  H  S  A  N  U  O
L  L  X  V  M  X  B  H  N  G  I  X  N  U  N
L  U  N  C  H  B  O  X  M  N  N  C  P  Y  H
L  T  B  I  F  B  P  R  N  F  I  Y  L  B  E
W  N  K  T  L  E  P  U  R  N  O  E  I  A  Q
X  F  M  Y  S  T  E  R  Y  T  K  N  Y  W  H
```

Word Bank

ANNIE	DOG	MISSING	SCHOOL
CAMERA	JASON	MYSTERY	
COOKIE	LUNCHBOX	PHOTOGRAPHIC	

Summary Program

At the end of a programming term, whether it is the end of the school year, the end of a semester or even the end of the programs in this book, a summary program is a good idea. A summary program gives the participants and group leader an opportunity to give closure to the book discussion group, receive feedback from the participants and measure the retention of the information covered. The following is an outline of a summary program that has proven successful.

Sample Summary Program

Program Preparation

At the second-to-the-last session, inform the participants that a graduation ceremony will occur at the last program. Each participant should bring in their favorite book and provide a brief (less than two minutes each) booktalk on his or her favorite book. Stress the fact that this is an opportunity to introduce others to what they personally enjoy. Point out that booktalks should be on books the reader thoroughly enjoyed; that the talker should pick an interesting event or character in the work or provide a brief summary of the entire work (without giving away the ending); and that the booktalk should be short.

The Day of the Program

When the day of the summary program arrives, provide copies of each of the books discussed in the book club. Provide a quick booktalk of each work, including the title, author and illustrator and a summary of the action. This is a perfect time to ask how many liked the selection and how many disliked the selection. The information gathered here can prove invaluable when repeating the program at a later date.

After you discuss each book, have the participants share their favorite works. Depending upon the size of your group, allow each participant two to three minutes to share his or her selection. If more than one child has picked the same book, encourage each one to complete his or her booktalk as planned (the reasons behind selecting a certain book are unique and it will also reinforce that it is acceptable to enjoy the same things but have different reasons as to why).

Book Bingo

After the children complete their individual booktalks, play Book Bingo, the memory evaluation stage of the summary program. Book Bingo asks the participants to remember certain details about each story in order to fill up their Bingo cards. The Book Bingo Questions on pages 71–73 include two questions from each story and answers to the questions. The questions can be mixed up or read in order. You may also add your own questions to the list. A blank Bingo card is provided on page 74. The children can play Bingo individually or in pairs. If possible, a book makes the perfect prize for Book Bingo, though bookmarks are wonderful substitutes and some fast food restaurants often provide bookmarks with coupons attached. Play until all participants win.

Book Bingo
Questions

- What is the name of the adopted boy in *A New Barker in the House?* **Marcos**

- What does Marcos from *A New Barker in the House* say when he wants to say hello? **hola**

- What was Amelia Earhart known for flying? **airplanes**

- Who was Eleanor Roosevelt married to? **President Franklin D. Roosevelt**

- Who has a photographic memory? **Cam Jansen**

- What was missing from Jason's lunch box? **a cookie**

- Who had a cold that caused him or her to blow houses down? **the wolf**

- Where was the wolf as he told his side of the story? **jail**

- What is the housekeeper's name in *Brothers of the Knight?* **Sunday**

- What kept wearing out in *Brothers of the Knight?* **shoes**

- What is the name of the dog in *Katie and the Sunflowers?* **Zazou**

- Who painted Katie's favorite painting? **van Gogh**

- What holiday did Dr. Pig create Porkenstein for? **Halloween**

- Who ate Dr. Pig's two brothers? **the Big Bad Wolf**

- What time of year did the little girl go owling in *Owl Moon?* **winter**

- Who took the little girl out to see an owl? **her father**

- Who fixed Dish in *And the Dish Ran Away with the Spoon?* **Jack**

- Who drew a map for Cat, Dog and Cow to help them find Dish and Spoon? **Fork in the Road**

- Who owns New Cat? **Mr. Kim**

- What is made at the factory where New Cat lives? **tofu**

- What instrument does Moses want to play when he grows up? **drums**

- What does Moses hold so he can feel the music? *a balloon*

- What kind of party is being thrown in *Mice and Beans?* **birthday**

- Who is throwing the birthday party in *Mice and Beans?* **Rosa María**

- What game does Casey play in *Casey at the Bat?* **baseball**

- Did the Mudville Nine win or lose the game in *Casey at the Bat?* **lose**

- Sam in *Sam and the Tigers* ate 169 what? **pancakes**

- What did the tigers turn into in *Sam and the Tigers?* **butter**

- Who gets the moon for Princess Lenore in *Many Moons?* **Jester**

- What does Princess Lenore want that makes her so sick in *Many Moons?* **the moon**

- Who enjoyed a meal of spaghetti and a shoelace? **Gregory**

- After Gregory's mom and dad took him to the dump to eat, what did Gregory get? **a stomachache**

- What is the name of the girl in *Goin' Someplace Special?* **'Tricia Ann**

- Where is 'Tricia Ann's someplace special? **the library**

- What direction is Tex moving in *Gila Monsters Meet You at the Airport?* **east**

- Who told the narrator of *Gila Monsters Meet You at the Airport* all the things he knew? **Seymour**

- Where does *Dumpling Soup* take place? **Hawaii**

- What is the celebration in *Dumpling Soup?* **New Year's Eve**

- What piece of computer equipment gives the father trouble in *Just the Two of Us?* **CD-ROM**

- What piece of clothing did the boy have taken away from him in *Just the Two of Us?* **his hat**

- Who led Joshua's family to freedom in *Journey to Freedom?* **Harriet Tubman**

- What was Joshua's family trying to escape? **slavery**

- What team did Aaron go see in *Matzah Ball*? **Baltimore Orioles**

- What was Aaron's dessert in *Matzah Ball*? **macaroons**

- What did May ride on to visit her grandmother? **train**

- What was May classified as in order to be mailed? **a baby chick**

- What did the ducks want from Farmer Brown in *Click, Clack, Moo*? **a diving board**

- What did the cows and chickens want from Farmer Brown? **electric blankets**

- What type of vehicle does Bust-'em-up Bill drive? **motorcycle**

- Where does Library Lil live? **Chesterville**

Book Bingo
Card

B	I	N	G	O

Answers to Puzzles

Amelia and Eleanor Go for a Ride
Crossword Puzzle

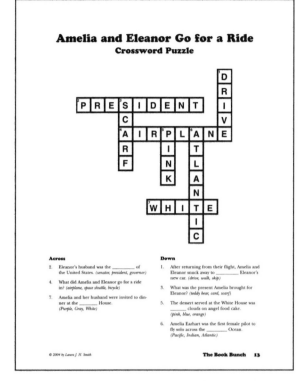

Across

2. Eleanor's husband was the _____ of the United States. (*senator, president, governor*)

4. What did Amelia and Eleanor go for a ride in? (*airplane, space shuttle, bicycle*)

7. Amelia and her husband were invited to dinner at the _____ House. (*Purple, Gray, White*)

Down

1. After returning from their flight, Amelia and Eleanor snuck away to _____ Eleanor's new car. (*drive, walk, skip*)

3. What was the present Amelia brought for Eleanor? (*teddy bear, card, scarf*)

5. The dessert served at the White House was _____ clouds on angel food cake. (*pink, blue, orange*)

6. Amelia Earhart was the first female pilot to fly solo across the _____ Ocean. (*Pacific, Indian, Atlantic*)

The Book Bunch 13

Click, Clack, Moo: Cows That Type
Word Search

Locate the words in the word bank. You will find the words up, down, across, diagonally or backwards.

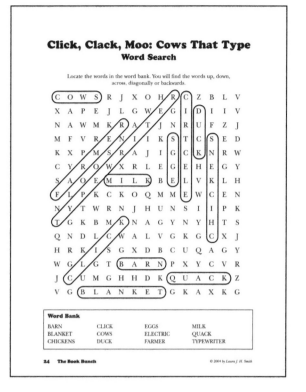

Word Bank

BARN	CLICK	EGGS	MILK
BLANKET	COWS	ELECTRIC	QUACK
CHICKENS	DUCK	FARMER	TYPEWRITER

24 **The Book Bunch**

Library Lil
Word Search

Locate the words in the word bank. You will find the words up, down, across, diagonally or backwards.

Word Bank

BILL	CHESTERVILLE	MOTORCYCLE	STORYTELLING
BOOKMOBILE	LIBRARY	PUPPETS	TELEVISION
BOOKS	LIL	STORM	

The Book Bunch 43

A New Barker in the House
Word Search

Locate the words in the word bank. You may find the words across or up and down.

Word Bank

BALL	FAMILIA	HOLA	SLIDE
BROTHER	FAMILY	PELOTA	SUBIBAJA
BUNNY	HELLO	SEESAW	SWING
COLUMPIO	HERMANA	SISTER	TOBOGAN
CONEJITO	HERMANO		

56 **The Book Bunch**

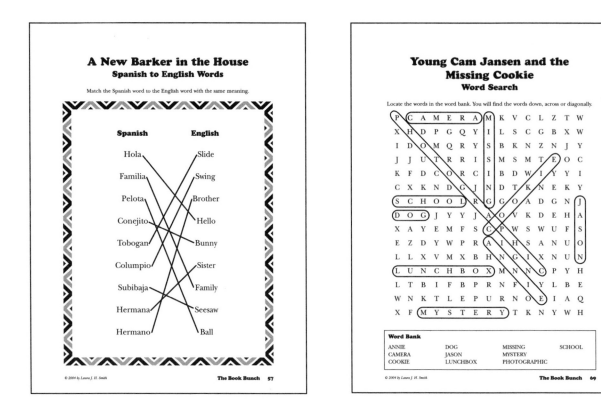

A New Barker in the House
Spanish to English Words

Match the Spanish word to the English word with the same meaning.

Spanish	English
Hola	Slide
Familia	Swing
Pelota	Brother
Conejito	Hello
Tobogan	Bunny
Columpio	Sister
Subibaja	Family
Hermana	Seesaw
Hermano	Ball

Young Cam Jansen and the Missing Cookie
Word Search

Locate the words in the word bank. You will find the words down, across or diagonally.

```
P C A M E R A M K V C L Z T W
X H D P G Q Y I L S C G B X W
I D O M Q R Y S B K N Z N J Y
J J U T R R I S M S M T E O C
K F D C O R C I B D W I Y Y I
C X K N D G J N D T K N E K Y
S C H O O L R G G O A D G N J
D O G J Y Y J A O V K D E H A
X A Y E M F S C P W S W U F S
E Z D Y W P R A I H S A N U O
L L X V M X B H N G I X N U N
L U N C H B O X M N N C P Y H
L T B I F B P R N F I Y L B E
W N K T L E P U R N O E I A Q
X F M Y S T E R Y T K N Y W H
```

Word Bank

ANNIE	DOG	MISSING	SCHOOL
CAMERA	JASON	MYSTERY	
COOKIE	LUNCHBOX	PHOTOGRAPHIC	

Index